All
Small

All Small

Poems by David McCord

Illustrations by Madelaine Gill Linden

Little, Brown and Company

Boston   Toronto   London

First Edition

Library of Congress Cataloging-in-Publication Data

McCord, David Thompson Watson, 1897—
  All small.

  Summary: Short and lively poems selected from
previous collections by the author.
  1. Children's poetry, American. [1. American poetry]
I. Linden, Madelaine Gill, ill. II. Title.
PS3525.A1655A6 1986   811'.52   85-19708
ISBN 0-316-55519-3
ISBN 0-316-55520-7 (pbk.)

HC: 10 9 8 7 6 5 4 3 2
PB: 10 9 8 7 6 5 4 3 2

WOR

All of these poems have appeared in the author's previous
collections, *All Day Long, Away and Ago, Far and Few,
For Me to Say, One at a Time,* and *Take Sky.*

*Published simultaneously in Canada
by Little, Brown & Company (Canada) Limited*

Printed in the United States of America

In Memory of
Annie Patterson Awalt
1891 — 1981
This book is dedicated to her daughters
Gladys J. Moulton,
Anna F. Thompson,
and her granddaughter
Katherine Thompson

Contents

The Door

Why is there more
behind a door
than there is
before:
kings,
things
in store:
faces,
places
to explore:
The marvelous shore,
the rolling floor,
the green man
by the sycamore?

Rain Song

The rain is driving silver nails
into the shingles overhead.
A little girl is playing scales;
she plays them as if something ails
her. Otherwise it's as I said:
The rain is driving silver nails
into the shingles overhead.

Secret

Jean said, *No.*
But Ruth said, *Yes!*
What? said Judy.
Gwyn said, *Guess!*
Where? said Karen.
There! said Claire.
But Lori's eyes said,
I don't care.

Innuendo

You are French? *Je suis.*
You speak French? *Mais oui.*
I don't speak French. *Non?*
I speak English. *Bon!*

Notice

I have a dog,
I had a cat.
I've got a frog
Inside my hat.

Crickets

all busy punching tickets,
clicking their little punches.
The tickets come in bunches,
good for a brief excursion,
good for a cricket's version
of travel (before it snows) to
the places a cricket goes to.
Alas! the crickets sing alas
in the dry September grass.
Alas, alas, in every acre,
every one a ticket-taker.

I Want You to Meet...

. . . Meet Ladybug,
her little sister Sadiebug,
her mother, Mrs. Gradybug,
her aunt, that nice oldmaidybug,
and Baby — she's a fraidybug.

Pome

Hlo
Outen myuncles varmule see
a nash a noak anna napple tree
an est three yeggs anna nold why ten
six sources scows buy a bigpigpen
pig skitten sand one colleap up
with lots ford inner yumyum sup
goobye

15

Lost

I have a little turtle
Name of Myrtle.
I have an extra lizard
Name of Wizard.
I have two kinds of snake:
Bill and Blake.
I have a dandy hutch
Without the rabbit.
If you see any such,
Will you please grab it?

Snail

This sticky trail
Was made by snail.
Snail makes no track
That he'll take back.
However slow,
His word is go.
(Twixt me and you
The word is goo.)

Cocoon

The little caterpillar creeps
Awhile before in silk it sleeps.
It sleeps awhile before it flies,
And flies awhile before it dies,
And that's the end of three good tries.

Glowworm

Never talk down to a glowworm —
Such as *What do you knowworm?*
How's it down belowworm?
Guess you're quite a slowworm.
No. Just say
        Helloworm!

Melvin Martin Riley Smith

Melvin Martin Riley Smith
Made do without what we do with.
For instance, did he have a kite?
He didn't, but he had the right
Amount of string to make one fly,
And lots and lots and lots of sky.

August 28

A flock of swallows have gone flying south;
The bluejay carries acorns in his mouth.
I don't know where he carries them or why.
I'm never sure I like the bluejay's cry,
But still I like his blue shape in the sky.

Knotholes

To make a knothole,
Knock out the knot;
And having a knothole,
What have you got?
You've got whatever
The fence shut in.
With lots of knots,
Where they have been
You've got whatever
The fence shut out.
You see what knotholes
Are all about?

The Cove

The cove is where the swallows skim
And where the trout-rings show,
And where the bullfrog hugs the rim
Of lily pads; and so
The million wake, as hatching flies
Hatch out into a world of eyes,
A world of wing and mouth and fin,
Of feathers, scales, and froggy skin.

A tough old world that *they* are in!

All Day Long

Beneath the pine tree where I sat
to hear what I was looking at,

then by the sounding shore to find
some things the tide had left behind,

I thought about the hilltop blown
upon by all the winds I've known.

Why ask for any better song
in all the wide world all day long?

Forget It

I'm not too sure that all I've read
Is under my hat or over my head;
What I've forgotten, so far as I see,
Is a matter between myself and me.
If things remembered since I was young
I don't keep right on the tip of my tongue,
It doesn't mean *something* won't come out!
What is it you want to know about?

Little

Little wind, little sun,
Little tree — only one.
Little bird, little wing,
Little song he can sing.
Little need he should stay,
Little *up*-now, away
Little speck, and he's far
Where all little things are.
Little things for me too:
Little sad that he flew.

Far Away

How far, today,
Is far away?
It's farther now than I can say,
It's farther now than you can say,
It's farther now than who can say,
It's very *very* far away:
You'd better better better play,
You'd better stay and play today.
Okay . . . okay . . . okay.

Wintry

Hylas in the spring,
Crickets in the fall:
In winter not a thing
To sing itself at all.

Fireflies follow May,
Bonfires Halloween;
Nothing lights up grey
Old winter in between.

Snowman

My little snowman has a mouth,
So he is always smiling south.
My little snowman has a nose;
I couldn't seem to give him toes,
I couldn't seem to make his ears.
He shed a lot of frozen tears
Before I gave him any eyes —
But they are big ones for his size.

Tomorrows

Tomorrows never seem to stay,
Tomorrow will be yesterday
Before you know.
Tomorrows have a sorry way
Of turning into just today,
And so . . . and so . . .

Something Better

We have a nice clean new green lawn,
And that's the one I'm playing on.
But down the street a little piece
There is a man who has three geese.
And when you see them, just beyond
You'll see a nice new deep blue pond.

Song

Wind and wave and star and sea,
And life is O! a song for me.
Wave and wind and sea and star,
Now I shall tell them what we are.
Star and sea and wind and wave,
I am a giant, strong and brave.
Sea and star and wave and wind,
You are the tiger I have skinned.